頑張って
GANBATTE

Wisconsin Poetry Series

Edited by Ronald Wallace and Sean Bishop

頑張って
GANBATTE

SARAH KORTEMEIER

THE UNIVERSITY OF WISCONSIN PRESS

The University of Wisconsin Press
728 State Street, Suite 443
Madison, Wisconsin 53706-1428
uwpress.wisc.edu

Gray's Inn House, 127 Clerkenwell Road
London EC1R 5DB, United Kingdom
eurospanbookstore.com

Printed in the United States of America
This book may be available in a digital edition.

Library of Congress Cataloging-in-Publication Data

Names: Kortemeier, Sarah, author.
Title: Ganbatte / Sarah Kortemeier.
Other titles: Wisconsin poetry series.
Description: Madison, Wisconsin : The University of Wisconsin Press,
    [2019] | Series: Wisconsin poetry series
Identifiers: LCCN 2019008581 | ISBN 9780299325145 (pbk. : alk. paper)
Subjects: | LCGFT: Poetry.
Classification: LCC PS3611.O7449 G36 2019 | DDC 811/.6—dc23
LC record available at https://lccn.loc.gov/2019008581

To those who welcome the stranger.

頑張って [ganbatte]

Japanese. Hold out, persevere, do your best.

CONTENTS

ACKNOWLEDGMENTS

So many people's generosities have made this book possible: I am grateful to Jane Miller, Barbara Cully, Maggie Smith, and Boyer Rickel (who modeled determination and kindness in a difficult season). This book took its initial form in conversation with the late Steve Orlen, who taught us all so much: we miss you, Steve.

I am deeply grateful to Carl Phillips, the Wisconsin Poetry Series, and the University of Wisconsin Press. Thank you for your belief in this work, and for all the work you do.

Thank you to the Intermenno Trainee Program, the Japan Exchange and Teaching Program, my cohorts who traveled with me, and the people who opened their homes, hearts, and lives to us all over the world. Many thanks to my dear friends and colleagues (past and present) at the University of Arizona and at the Poetry Center: Tucson writers hold each other up. Heartfelt gratitude to my parents, who showed me how to make art out of life every day of my childhood; to my brother, who carries on the tradition; and to Keith, who is the center.

Grateful acknowledgments are due to the editors of the following publications in which these poems first appeared (some in slightly different form).

Alaska Quarterly Review: "Day Trip"
Barrow Street: "Gretel"
Folio: "The Holdout"
The Feminist Wire: "Stone with Nineteen Corners"
Journal of Mennonite Writing: "Amsterdam," "Mt. Fuji Is Still Active," "Poem [I didn't want to speak . . .]," "First Week," and "[namaru]"
Pilgrimage: "[itadakimasu]"
Ploughshares: "[hodos]" and "The Dark Constellations"
Sentence: "Inheritance" and "[I visited]"
"Expatriate" first appeared in *Fairy Tale Review* (*The Emerald Issue*), ed. Kate Bernheimer and Timothy Schaffert, Detroit, MI: Wayne State University Press, 2014.

頑張って
Ganbatte

Preface

認める [mitomeru]. *Japanese. To recognize, appreciate, observe, notice. Radical:* 言, *speech.*

Wahrnehmen. *German. To notice, sense, perceive. Literal translation: "to take for truth."*

There are interiors I can't photograph.

My boss in Hannover and her endless polishing. Wine glasses, name tags.

Practice sessions. Before the festival, we'd meet in a shrine cleared of its statues and play the drums. Takashi brought extra sake so I'd be welcome.

Practice sessions. I sang Brahms over the dishes and memorized the words for "maiden," "iron," "guarded," "transform."

A friend who tried to sing in the Hiroshima museum.
A charred lunch box with a placard underneath.

I am an amateur.
I have to look.
Without the photos, all I have are catalogs.

The calendar and Pocky wrappers in Satomi's kitchen.
The afternoons falling blue across the table.

A pile of empty suitcases in a room at the Auschwitz museum.
A tag with a name printed on it, pressed up against the glass.

The way Satomi said my name at the end
of nearly every sentence, with an *ah* in it,
and a hiss.
The lift of an eyelid as she nodded.
She nodded constantly,
like an interviewer.

ὁδός [hodos]

Greek. 1. A traveled way, a road. 2. A traveler's way; journey.

The idea of a woman as a road
has a certain appeal: I think of setting off
along myself, boots sucking softly
at the mud.

The Greeks imagined the uterus hiking
up and down. The booted
empty uterus, sniffing for blood.

And the virgin oracle set a stool
above a volcano, and squatted down,
and Apollo entered her through the vented fumes.
The two of them churned the road
together, until the mud was dust
and her womb cried out with a memory
of what had never happened. And then,
as she floated, hysterical, inside herself, the god
would fill her jaws, and speak.

I think of a trail crumbling off a cliff in Hawaiʻi,
a charred bicycle tire in a Hiroshima museum,
a page from a diary displayed behind glass with its own
special lamp.
Journeys penetrate. Afterward, song
and the stench of burning from things
we thought were private.

Gretel

is hungry all the time. When she shares
the bread with her brother, she notes approvingly
how hungry she still is. She imagines the birds
gulping the crumbs she's left behind, the browned-off bits
of crust catching and rasping in their throats,
and thinks, *At least I know how to chew.*
You see? she says aloud. *See what?* her brother says.
Gretel thinks of houses, of the ovens she will light,
the dough she will smash and stretch.
The path, she tells her brother.

Hansel

is lost and likes it,
likes the way the forest's
shadows do not submit
to maps. He shrugs
at Gretel and her games:
This bush is the front door,
she says as they sit down,
this log my tea table.
He looks to the spaces
between the trees.
Whatever is empty can erupt.
I see
nothing, he says, and pounds with heat.

秋 [aki]

Japanese. Autumn.

Blue. A holding
of breath. Trees shrink away from
their portion of fire.

Poem

I didn't want to speak, because everybody has,
because my grief has no surprises. But I went
to Manhattan, later, and there was a chain-link fence
between the people and the hole. You could press your face
right up, get your eyelashes past the wire.
Push the most flickering and delicate parts of the body
(pupil, lid) into negative space.

A child outside a restaurant waves her hands and wails.
Bonnie, look at the step, her father chides. *It's two
and a quarter inches down.*
The child stares at the curb.
*If you want to be carried, use
your words.*

We have no photos of them climbing up to windowsills.
We could not justify such photographs. We can barely
justify the songs.

In the guestbook at the Hiroshima Peace Memorial Museum,
an American has written: *Sorry you started the war. Glad
we finished it.* Outside, my friend and I begin to sing
"Dona nobis pacem," but stop because we feel
self-conscious.

In New York, they mark the minutes of impact with silence
every year. In the news photographs, everybody leans:
head on hand, hand on fence.
In the face of silence, sometimes I revert to postures I've seen
in movies, or from my parents.

The young German on the train is frank with me: *Look,*
we feel terrible about it. But we didn't do it. It's not
our generation.

In the photo that stays with me, a baby frowns up at her mother
while smoke unfolds in the skyscrapers behind. The mother wears
a black tank top, and the shadow of the photographer lies
along her back, slipping along the spaghetti strap, almost edging
underneath. Shadow on skin. Overhead, the fires,
the man, the camera.
She does not look up.

Objectives

The light in the airport
the three of them dark against a window
my brother the tallest shadow
my parents curly and broader

The blond boy beside me on the plane
his German vocabulary notes in a blue book
he shows me *Augenblick*
(moment)
the mustard sauce and the smell of cushions
Greenland under the wing
in his notebook he writes another word
mutterseelenallein (lit. abandoned
even by the soul of your mother;
all alone)

The blond boy buys a car
we drive all night
I take his hand and forget what to do with it
he is more humid than I
and the morning, gray as an airport, cracks open
over the ferry in its dock
the boat about to become
its own reflection, sliding white across the morning calm
the deer on this island expect to be fed

And so we cross to Denmark
simply to cross to Denmark
we buy duty-free Toblerones
and cross back to Germany

the sun shines on the water
we've left behind
blond boy I will not come to bed
and the ferry slips back and forth

First Week

My new house had a rice maker, a big bed, a water heater, two tables, and no towels.
Ito-sensei brought me two wrapped in cellophane. *I*
have
new towels at
my house, she explained—very slowly—when I asked,
since you have to have
new towels for
your guests.
One skin per towel.
When the guests leave, the towels are thrown out.

Ito-sensei brought
me to her house. The door was made of some
dark, dark wood.

Her mother and father bowed to me.

It's not the right word.
I mean they crooked their bodies, kneeling, their foreheads on the mat.

I moved like something very warm, very large.
A savanna concentrating toward a single drop of rain.

I met my desk in the Board of Education.
I drafted drawings for the children who were about to visit their sister school
    in Wisconsin. *What's*
different
that they should know about? Ito-sensei asked me.
All I could remember was the way you don't shower all over the floor in
    American bathrooms. Keep
the curtain inside the bathtub, I said, and *H* stands for *Hot.*

This is my story, I hummed. *This is my song.*

Another expat told me about a German sausage restaurant in Miyoshi.
And wait'll you hear its name: St. Schwein.
He walked three miles, through several tunnels under hills and through
the sea air, to tell me this.

I had no oven. I adapted all my chicken for the stovetop. My mother's cookies
    arrived in the mail.
I hoarded them all the way to Thailand.

I photographed flowers and walls.

I did not take the train to Tokyo for the weekend.
I did not join the local choir. There was a welcome
party. Ito-sensei bought me a $20 piece of sushi.
I don't remember its name.

I went to the 7-Eleven at sunset. Sometimes you could see Mount Fuji
from that hill, if the wind blew hard at the city air,
if the light was gone enough.

You could get everything at a 7-Eleven in Japan. Including
a bill for your electricity.

I saw you walking
yesterday, a student said, and looked at me
as though I were a word in French
or a leaning mountain, far away.

Stimmtausch

German. In music, a voice exchange.

I walk to the grocery store, practicing.

The language I need is always at the bottom *yo quisiera je voudrais ich möchte* and I cycle until finally I arrive at -たいです. Along the way there's just enough time to toss out a pseudointellectual meditation on my Eurocentric bias and while I'm there I run some other verbs and add in objects おいしい寿司が食べたいです I am feeling excessively fluent today; when I think fast enough to attach です at the end I know I'm really wailing. And in any case I pretty much always want to eat delicious sushi, right, so this is a good sentence to have at the top of the rummage heap; holy shit I'm only walking to the grocery store but *I am in Japan was für ein Abenteuer*; no, go away, you are not helping; *il pleure dans mon coeur*; you're not either and aren't we dramatic today? but here's the supermarket. OK.

Cilantro or Italian parsley wrapped in clear plastic. Scentless. I can't read the signs.

So ask somebody.

Cilantroを買いたいですが

Cilantro わ

I don't know the word for cilantro.

Eggs Benedict for dinner, then. Again.

***

The first character I learned in Japanese was 火山, "fire mountain": volcano. There are other words with fire inside them when they are written down:
Refine. Autumn. Brave. Tuesday.

Surveillance

We already know we're watched.
When we water the tomato plant,
spread ourselves along the couch with one leg up.
When we slide the bra strap
back underneath the shirt. When we lean
to breathe in hair. When we pass a bank
and whisper to each other. When we put on
our ski masks and burst through the doors,
there is something watching us.
Please, something, watch us.

Tourist

I

The jellyfish pulses toward the surface as the day fades. Water in. Water out.
It has no idea who it is, but it knows
disturbance. Ships' captains, between transactions,
see it glowing in the wake.

II

This is what comes of lonely planets and NPR.
This is what comes of trying on blouses, trying on languages,
temples, rice fields. After I take the photos,
I turn for home. Home is where
I tug my shirt off. Where the mirrors are.
The stains of color in the closet, where
I leak a little into my jackets. Every day.

III

But sometimes the postcards are sort
of true. Red roof on a hill in the sun.

Squid in gold sauce. Tight jeans. An icon
with the Madonna's left breast

lithe in the mouth of the Child.
I buy a little piece

of glass for a necklace. I tell myself
it's a gift for a friend. Meanwhile, I wear it,

a sudden brightness at the throat as from
a hymn, or as from blood, an outpouring

that can't be taken back again.

The Grail

I. Stonehenge
I am twenty-three, and the circle is too old to be convincing:
stones on an abandoned
hillside. I assume an inhabited hillside
within myself.

II. Cadair Idris
The mountain's name means *seat of Idris,*
Idris the giantish bard who used one of its lakes
as an armchair. To spend the night up there
is to risk madness—or poetry.
There is too damn much fog
on the path.

III. Dinas Brenin
is a hill by a road.
There is always more underbrush than I expect
between me and the ruins. I get off
the bus. I look up. I get on
the bus. There was blood here. A dragon, if you brush
the stories too close. The new asphalt on the highway,
the sunny normalcy of the sky
make words like "lair" embarrassing.
In good weather, there are no hiding places left.

IV. Salisbury Cathedral

Weather scrapes the cathedral's
outer walls. On the threshold, I shake
off rain. The green men watch
from odd angles.

They're carved in hidden places: north
of the high altar, at the base of a pillar, on the corner
of a tomb.

Some of the faces are barely human: branches burst
from ears, from noses, eyes. They have given in
to renaissance.

V. Carn March Arthur

The print of Arthur's horse
is a knot in a stone. The lake
from which Arthur whirled
his monster, a pond. The wind is gray
and very cold. But the pond
echoes the estuary in the valley below.
There is a sea beyond that. A homecoming. A color.

冬 [fuyu]

Winter
doesn't mean
anything but winter. Fold
it neatly and try not to look its way,
as though it were
the coat of a friend who betrayed you.

Home

The tiki head I brought back from New Zealand
stands for no one's death in particular,
no one's particular face.
Eyes of abalone, eyes of insomnia.
My mother moves it, month to month,
living room to stairs to kitchen.
My father so much thinner.
Over dinner, we practice the rounds
we sang when I was a child:
Dona nobis pacem.
I will arise and go unto my father.
Who'll buy my roses? Who'll buy my posies?
My mother so much thinner,
my father rinsing off her plate
when she puts her utensils down.
We wish. We wish, we wish.

The First House

I've had this dream before. I am skiing
somewhere silver, somewhere foreign
and sharply mountained. The early winter moonrise
hangs round me like a wedding dress. Snow whispers
under the skis: *This is something only you can do.*
Across the ridge, a light bulb flashes out between the pines.
I will count the people in these homesteads, count them all,
these dark-coated people who so seldom see a stranger,
who so seldom are surprised.

The first house, when it comes, comes quickly.
A curtain shifts. The light that falls across the snow
looks like urine, looks like rage. The door
cries out when I pound.

Expatriate

Ausländerin. *German. Foreigner; outside-country woman.*

外国人 [gaikokujin]. *Japanese. Foreigner; outside-country person.*

I lack this courage: to walk barefoot in a nightgown
through the grass. To stand in my own
garden and think, *I planted this. Tomorrow, we will eat.*

I have a picture in my head
of a surfer's shadow interrupting moonlight
on foam, though that's too dangerous
to be real. The summer can't end.

We know the Beijing Wall was built for defense.
We tend not to realize it's a small mountain range.

In my photograph, his face
is tangled in leaf shadows.
The wooden recorder at his lip
holds back song. Arrests
our long glissando into the grass.

There is something to be gained from the boar
who comes trampling through my corn.
For one, there is his neck,
throbbing and scratching at my elbows
as I hurl myself to catch him.
For another, there is his breath,
hot with escape. I dig in my heels.

需 [ju]

Japanese. Need; demand.

An old woman and a wheelbarrow
on the margin of the road, her back a hook,
her garden upright. Her granddaughter scraped
out and remembered on the mountain:
a shrine, a tree, a red bib comforting
the neck of a short statue. The old woman pours
secret water over the stony head, prays the soul
will cross the river. The radishes swell, the rice floods,
the rake soaks up the rain.

Poem

Mitteilen. *German. To communicate; literal translation "to part with" [root verb* teilen. *to part, divide, intersect].*

The walls in the Anne Frank house are yellow. Old water.
Outside, the blue of the day. A diary page inside a glass case:
Oh, I'm so glad I brought you along.

Back at work in Germany, Frau Merz is telling a story.
Es war ein Baby, she says. *The baby was new
as a bomb*, I think. Similes are the expatriate's
most terrible habit.

A morning in Thailand, after Christmas, after
the wave. I meet a girl whose friends
had a tent on the beach at Phuket.
The breakfast mangoes arrive. The Red Cross
already has more blood than it can handle.
She sits at a computer, refreshing the page.

Mount Fuji Is Still Active

At first I thought the *san* you attach to the ends
of mountain names in Japanese was the same
as the honorific: *Good evening, Fuji-san.*
I will climb you now. To drink
a traditional sunrise from the summit
of the old volcano, you begin the climb after supper
with tourists, locals, boys and their knees,
Japanese women in black skirts
and heels. This is not to say that Fuji is an easy
hike. The saying goes, *Everyone should climb Mount Fuji*
once; only an idiot would climb it twice.

But I don't remember a single face.
Now, when I think about the shadow we climbed,
much bigger than the strip of stars we barely
glanced at overhead—The line of the mountain's
flank was always ahead of us, do you see?
And the terror lay in its slowness, the way it rose
mere steps at a time and still drowned out
the sky. We never saw the sun come up.
There was light, and a simmering pot
of clouds, and utter inhumanity.
I don't like heights. But still.
Sometimes I wish I'd never learned the language.

Inheritance

For my father

A man stands at the water's edge in the gray of the afternoon and shouts. His boat has overturned. His hair drips. He shouts for his drowned father.

This same man stands in yellow light. It is evening in a church. He is singing, and these are the words: *You haven't an eye, you haven't a leg, halloo! Halloo! Johnny, I hardly knew ye.* An old woman corrects her blouse and whispers. *I don't think he should sing war songs here.*

The man is on another stage. He is Titus Andronicus. The lights are blue and his daughter's robes are white. He breaks her neck, as she has asked him to do. He shakes and the light shakes with him.

いただきます [itadakimasu]

Japanese. Expression of gratitude, said before eating.

The festival floats
down the dark stone road: the drummers
in night-colored coats, the toddlers
in celebration braids, Takashi's daughter
brushing aside kimono sleeves
to aim her camcorder. The beer began
at 8 a.m., and now the rope
is dusky in our hands; the shrine bumps,
immortal, half-forgotten, behind us.
When we stop, the children dance
to the flute in masks that make them older.
The last of today's meals waits for us at the cemetery:
sake, fried chicken, rice, chocolates, fish,
but the wives will already be gone, their weekend's
work cooling under the torches.
For us now, as we take our seats
next to the still stone crowd, there is only
the humming of blood, the still-closed door
between our drunkenness and our dying.

Fleißig

Meaning work done well, and quickly.
You'll say *efficient*, and I won't quite
let you: work that is *efficient* isn't
beautiful. It lacks a straightness
to the hem of the tablecloth, an extra sparkle
in the wine glass.

House and hill and butcher shop.
Cobbles, laid down so cleanly
the gaps are still sharp. Add
cleanliness to the list:
work done well, quick, clean.
Crumbs brushed away.

The bridge in Heidelberg is one
thousand years old. I am sitting on it.

Fleißig the dawn.
Fleißig the *Apfel*.
Fleißig the brown tea I have not let blacken. *Fleißig* the crowded feet on the tram.
Fleißig the *ehrlich gesagt*. *Fleißig* Ritter chocolate. *Fleißig* the grass between the
    baker's and the train station.
Fleißig the hole in my jeans. *Fleißig* the genitive case, for which I made up a
    mnemonic rap song.
Fleißig the *Irre*, the madness that overtakes me when I sing hymns. *Fleißig* the
    jar to keep honey in. The *Kapellmeister* with his back to the empty pews.
    The language in which I learn to "jinx" before I learn to "finish."
Fleißig the nearby castle. *Fleißig* the dent in its wall. The prayer in the breeze: *sei
    geliebte.* Be beloved. *Fleißig* the queerness of it, the sitting-downness of it.
Fleißig the seams in the field. The tray with the candle to keep the tea hot.
Fleißig the upper-class ticket to Berlin. The valleys in my shoe.

Fleißig the Wall.

Fleißig the air that moves over.

Fleißig the boy who shrugged when I asked him the time.

Fleißig the crumbs of the Wall I've saved in my suitcase.

Fleißig the graffiti: Help Me, God, to survive this deadly love. Fight Your
   Misery. Test the Best.

Fleißig Johanna and the red bobbles on her scarf.

Fleißig the kid she was, growing up on the wrong side. The liquor she buys me
   as she tells stories.

Fleißig die Mauer, she might say.

Fleißig the new tampons in the grocery when *die Mauer* came down, she does say.

Fleißig the orange rags she used to strap between her legs, I say.

Fleißig the open rain. The pressure of my mother's hands on the sofa. The quiet
   in the study. The room I crept to, not understanding. The soul of the TV
   news, which failed to follow me upstairs. The ten-year-old I was in 1989,
   the terrible indifference.

Fleißig the amends.

Fleißig my blinks and my silence. *Fleißig* the lower windows in Dresden.

Fleißig early morning at the Anne Frank house. *Fleißig* the wooden chair near
   her bed.

Fleißig the full lobby in the art museum.

Fleißig the *irgendwo*. The wherever to which we travel.

Fleißig the music in the Walkman. The nap on the train headed east.

Fleißig the Polish town whose name I do not quite pronounce correctly. The
   quiet gas, which none of us smelled. The realm of the suitcase, discarded.
   The sign with a name on it, which we do not understand.

We do not know what is a name and what is a story.

Fleißig the tenth bale of human hair.

Don't worry. There is glass between us and the bale.

Day Trip

It looks like the States, someone murmurs,
and we stare at the wideness of the road, the space
spent on boulevards. Where Tokyo
has multiple stories of everything, lights
and stairwells and alleys that twist
against themselves like human intestines,
Hiroshima is drivable. It has space
for the sun to expand.
We've been told to try the *okonomiyaki* here,
a word that means *whatever you like,*
grilled. The Peace Park is the greenest space
in this plant-loving city. They've hung chains
of origami on a rod, so that the chains
and chains of paper cranes look like jackets in party colors,
clothes for a manic phase. Think your hometown pride
parade. Think "Joseph and the Amazing Technicolor
Dreamcoat." Think of something else. We try to sing
for the cranes, *dona nobis*, and here we begin
to see the false beauty of harmony, give us,
give us, as if singing will bring us
pacem.

In the museum, a lunch box.
It's open and black. Inside, the placard says,
it held some rice. I'm pretty sure there was
some fish as well. I remember the color, the mass, the blacks.
I can't see the child without the mess
that's left of her meal, the crumbling fuzz
of ash, the shadows of stains. The opened locks.

Okonomiyaki

turns out to be a savory pancake. Mine has egg
and squid and a breath of something
terribly familiar.

口

[I visited]

I visited Auschwitz by myself when I was twenty-three. It was intense, I tell people when they ask. Can't really be quantified in words. This gets me out of having to explain what I didn't learn.

You see a mound of hair, I mean a ten-by-twenty-foot mountain of fuck-me-that's-all-fucking-*hair*, and there is nothing to be done with it. You curse a lot; you feel that this somehow shows respect. You circle it. You re-observe what you learned in kindergarten about playdough:

all those colors mixed together look kind of gray. You remember your father making a gray playdough man for his graduate movement class and holding his arm in front of him. You remember how he was his own model.

[We can't refuse]

We can't refuse to write: to make notes is to *do* something. We choose to observe: it is a matter of control, though the control may be an illusion.

. . . Check for gold teeth . . . There was [sic] almost 2,000 kilograms of women's hair . . . The Nazis used it as a base for textiles: you could buy it for 50¢ per kilogram.

I reread my journal notes on the Auschwitz trip. In places, I have commented on my feelings. For most of the entry, however, I have faithfully plagiarized the guide's speech. This recitation is the only part of the entry that is honest.

The tour guide said that the corpses were usually found in layers: strong adults on top, children on the bottom, I wrote. I probably thought I was trying to memorize it. It didn't work: years later, I have to rediscover these things as I dig up the little notebook I carried around Europe. The notebook is lined with leather. I don't know what type of skin it is. *The poison used to gas prisoners was in capsule form; it only became gas at 37 degrees C, so when the SS dropped the pellets into the gas chambers, the body heat of the prisoners was sufficient to convert it into gas.*

The handwriting does not deviate.

You're literally standing on the ashes strewn near the Birkenau crematoria. Some of the gray, gritty soil got into my sandals, I wrote, then: *and instead of feeling creeped out, I rather felt it as an honor.* This is a lie.
Say "privilege," intending the double meaning, and perhaps it might come closer to truth. Or perhaps not.

At the end of this journal entry, I have left one line blank.

Below it, I have made another note. *Tu hai culo!—You the ass, you have an ass! (You rock!)*
I do not now remember which language this was in.

語 [go]

Japanese. Language

has two mouths.
One for speech   one for sound
one explains   one hammers flat

home (that plumpness in the mind)
modulates into silent distances

For Emphasis

Oh, you darling time,
you can exclaim in German.
Anything can be smaller.
Oh, my little God.

Some vulgarities are much like ours—
kommen means *to come,* in both its senses;
verdammt, verpiss, and *ficken* mean
exactly what you think.

Some are not. *Go fuck your knee,*
you could say, optimistically.
Kids say *horny* where we say *awesome,*
sometimes with intensifiers: *mega-horny like*
a sow. Anything can mate:
where we say *henpecked,* they say *slipper-master.*
Where we say *douche,* they say *you ass-violin.*

My German friends didn't want to teach me these.
Here, at home, that's all they want to know.

[There is a Gucci]

There is a Gucci bag in every car on the Yamanote Line in Tokyo. The most beautiful scarf I have ever seen on a human was wound around the neck of a woman who grew up on the eastern side of the Berlin Wall. A red scarf with dangly parts—a crude and easy metaphor. When a Japanese woman cut my hair, she layered everything until it no longer moved. Sleek, that's what I was, but I still had wrong angles.

These wars are older, and people are careful to tell you only the good stuff. My boss in Japan loves the Green Bay Packers, wears white Nikes with a gray suit. The legend of the kamikaze, he tells me, is that they murmured *Mother* as the planes went down. Frau Merz remembers her skirt coming off in the snow—*I was trying to hold the baby in,* she chortles.

I gain some weight, and Frau Merz laughs some more. *Everything here has cream in it.* I lose some weight, and my boss congratulates me at lunch. *That's good,* he says in Japanese, and all the teachers nod. *Sarah-san got incredibly fat when she came to Japan.* I am a goodwill ambassador. Every so often, I mop the floor. Every so often, I'm lent a kimono. At karaoke, I sing about the delicious rabbits of someone else's hometown. At the Bierbörse, I learn a drinking song about ham and egg sandwiches. We buy food, we buy beer, my boss slides into my lap, we have money for cabs, the trains are running; is there time to outgrow these clothes?

訛る[namaru]

When I speak, I transform.
Ningen (a person) to *ninjin* (a carrot):
we are all carrots here together,
I tell the teachers, weeping
a little into my school lunch.
I thump chopsticks against the tray
and earnestly call them stars.
To scoop up enchantment
with a spoon: to mispronounce.

Poem

Abstand. *German. Distance; space; gap.*

My roommate's mother
sent a homemade Advent calendar
to our apartment in Germany.
Cookies crumbling behind
their silver doors.
German's quite easy, my roommate
told me. *The grammar's all the same, you know.*

A woman found me in a parking lot
at a Japanese chain store.
She said, *Do you speak English?*
I think we should be friends.
I went home instead.
You watched My Neighbor Totoro *last night,*
a student told my friend.
She'd seen the movie through his living
room window. Sometimes, people followed
me around the grocery store to see
what I'd put in my cart.

My German roommate did not attend my wedding.
My parents talk of retiring to New Zealand.

Satomi, didn't you have another baby?
I'm looking for the painting you gave me
of the *mikaeri-bijin*:
the beautiful woman looking back over her shoulder,
a famous theme. She must be in a drawer somewhere.
She's been lost for years.
Satomi still teaches English *juku.*
Her students email me, though she does not.

My German roommate and I found a model
skeleton in the kitchen. I don't know why
the kitchen had a skeleton. We dressed it
up for Halloween. We put a boa over its bare pelvis.
I wore a kimono to graduation at the Japanese junior high.
Ningyou mitai, said my boss:
You look
like a doll.

[They seem]

They seem to like two-story houses with children inside. Clapboard, private bedrooms.

Occasionally you'll hear about them at railroad crossings. The landscapes of childhood may be a key to the mystery, then: you don't find ghosts in the boardroom.

Ghosts move in to abandoned places, to houses and stretches of wood with no real story. They are not generally allowed to displace historical narratives. The Anne Frank Annex in Amsterdam is not said to be haunted, though her handwriting still covers the wallpaper and the daylight moves very slowly across the wooden floor.

Ghosts open the kitchen door and close it again. When you are searching for a notebook, ghosts place it in the center of a table as you turn your back. Ghosts come to you in a dark mirror if you chant their names, if you believe loud enough.

My mother:
I'm seeing columns now, white columns, in my mind's eye. They called it the old slave house. I think there was a breeding operation going on. They kept a big guy up in the third floor, fathering babies for future profit. I was only in seventh grade, but I felt it. Cold.

My friend:
I would wake up and I'd see all four of them standing over me. They never did anything or made any noise. They just watched.

My college boyfriend took me to a railroad crossing on the South Side of San Antonio. The crossing was set in an embankment. You drove up and over the tracks and down the other side. If you stopped the car before you reached the upward slope to the track and took your foot off the brake, the car would move up and over the tracks on its own. I don't know if a train really sliced open a school bus full of children on those tracks. But my car did move. Where there is empty space, an afternoon alone in the sun, a foot taken from a brake, we pull the watchers closer.

[In 2002, the mark]

In 2002, the mark had just given way to the euro in Germany, and Frau Kappel shook her head over everything. Chocolate: no. Blue jeans: no. Tram fares: no. A euro is worth twice a mark, she said to me, and now they're charging €2 for an apple that used to cost DM 2. This sort of transaction was all I could understand of her speech: my roommate, who spoke marvelous, liquid German, translated everything else. Frau Kappel would smile at me and her whole face would go thin. At first I only saw the effort.

Frau Kappel was Russian, as were several other women who worked with us in the conference center kitchen. She married a German sometime after the war. Our head cook remembered the American GIs coming through with guns and gum in their pockets. The head cook seemed younger than Frau Kappel; he had an authoritative stomach. Frau Kappel was already starting to bend over in the characteristic crouch of the old, her hands, like her smile, stretched to starvation point, mimicking the forced and brittle curvature of her back.

"Kalinka" came on the kitchen radio every day between 4:00 and 4:30 p.m. The lyrics to "Kalinka" are the only Russian words I know, so I'd sing it with her—probably the longest conversations we had. I have the image of her hands, bouncing up and down, as though she were trying to conduct my performance of the song, and that thin smile again, as though she'd just repeated a word for the ninth time and was waiting for me to pronounce it wrong again.

My roommate and I received five weeks of paid vacation time from the dishwashing and the vegetables. Frau Kappel and the other kitchen workers got six. I told her about my summer job, translating Bible verses. My roommate had to interpret most of it for me, and I could see Frau Kappel didn't really believe it. At home, I told her, we're lucky if we get two weeks off all year. Frau Kappel didn't believe this either. *But everybody says America is so lovely*, she said. The day before my roommate and I left, there was a party. Everybody said something. About me, Frau Kappel said, *She can work.*

I don't remember if we ever asked her about the war. It seems to me a conversation that would not have prospered. Whenever I remember her, she is aiming herself with speed and intensity, with a precise mouth, carrying casserole from the kitchen out to the waiting guests.

時 [ji]

Japanese. Time.

The temple next to the day,
never touching
     but
             young leaves breathe
on wooden pillars.
       Raindrops glitter in the camera flash.

Crouching before a bronze Buddha
      larger than home
          still   still   and we're shaking with it
               knowing the collapse will come
                   knowing the mud with our feet

[She becomes]

She becomes a statue. She becomes a metal. She crouches over a metal child. The mouth about to open. The viewer invited to supply grammar in her own mother tongue. Contractions. The statue's arms elided into the body of her son. The bronze chest and thighs curled around. The placard elliptical. "Statue of Mother and Child in the Storm." The flesh about to melt to its component hydrogens.

The bronze is green with weather.
You may touch it.

You are hungry, but this would be tasteless to mention now. In Hiroshima, everything you do has a backdrop of wide boulevards, green spaces between the traffic. Tree/pause. The streets are gridded. Regular stops at lights. It is like Chicago, it is like New York. New. Streets new. Red/pause.

Look at the statue. You see that she has another child. Two children. One is in her arms. The other is trying to climb her from the back. To protect her, or distract her. Subordinate clauses.
You diagram the sentence. You pull out a map. The city's memory hot in your hair.

Underneath the layer of corrosion, the metal is protected: she will never turn to dust. You won't swallow her. Speak all you want.

って

Kyoto

Onions sizzling. A dark room, a griddle, bright glasses of beer.
A river with an arched wood bridge.

A schoolgirl's blue skirt.
The rumor of a geisha, the lovely absence in the hot afternoon.

Three round stones in a stream.
Power lines on a gray street.

A highway of tiny lanterns and a red gate over a shrine.
The standard greeting from the children on the school trip: *Hello! Do you have*
a pen?

The cars shout on the street.
The leaves drift on the moat.

Everyone has the same photo of Kinkakuji: the glow
of the golden temple reflected in the lake, the blitzed smiles.

The cell phones are lifted, the cherry trees bloom
like blizzards in a season when snow is impossible.

Amsterdam

whitish afternoon, check-in at the hostel
red chill-out cushion as big as your living room
Jeff Buckley in the air with the smoke
long blue ticket with holes punched for each tram ride
french fry restaurant with the curry sauce and special mayonnaise
bikes massed in the parking garage at the train station
red brick of the station, big clock
red light behind the woman in the window
white ruffles and skin
smooth hair might be brown
remembering it without a photo is difficult
the painting at the end of a long, long hall in the museum
the pouring of milk from a jug, blue undertones in the paint
outside, a man skids past on a bicycle
color warring with itself in the Van Gogh museum
orange and red fragmenting the winter light

The Anne Frank House is like the rest of the city: connected
to itself.
The east wall of the house is also the west wall of the next.
The floor is still the same wood planking.
The scribblings are there, pencil on wallpaper.
Rocking chair bent after half a century.
The red plaid of the diary cover now pinked a little.

It's stored outside the annex proper
in a display case surrounded by gray tile and plate windows.
So much daylight.
The handwriting collapses to one side.
The whole annex yellow, as if sweat-stained.
In her room, photos all over the yellow walls.
Most frame a woman's face, any woman's face.
They all have dark hair.
They are speechless and young.
They take the place of windows.

平安 [heian]

Japanese. Peace.

An old man calligraphing
as the rain blows through an unclosed window
to freckle his untouched tea.
On the page in front of him,
the character echoes:
under the flat surface of old grief,
a roof. Under the roof,
a woman.

Stone with Nineteen Corners

There is a stone with nineteen corners
in one of Machu Picchu's walls.

The builders fit the wall
around the nineteen corners, thinking

in three dimensions at once.
They made a thing that has too many turns

to fit inside a photograph.
The scholars think they did it to show off.

Other tourists claim the stone has thirty corners,
or thirty-two corners, or twelve, or nine. We didn't

count them ourselves;
our guides managed us. The long-dead builders

manage us. The stone exists;
it hides parts of itself from every

line of sight; still, we rest against the wall
and look down at the valley, we go ahead

and take the photos, we submit to frames,
we make them ourselves, we carry

our children and look back at the honeymoon
photos, thinking, *There was so much light*

up there, thinking, *What was that guy's
name?*, thinking, *I'd like to see it again.*

頑張って [ganbatte]

Japanese. Hold out, persevere, do your best.

the all-pink karaoke sign
the afternoons spent in a square of sun, the lit tatami mat
the Asahi gold in the glass, the tatami gold underfoot, the gold light on gold foil
aftertaste of tang from a green onion
ads in the supermarket: "Very Soft Meat." "Men's Pocky."
adzuki beans dripping from a stick
air at the town festival, gold with candles and blue with sundown
the allegiance to blood type: A is sensitive, B is rowdy
American elections on TV, curiosity: *Why Bush again?*

bamboo on every hill
bright water in the rice paddy
breakfast sun reflected in the rice water
balls of mochi sticking to the index finger
the British guy and his bloody hells
the broken wine glass

cold water when I forget to ask how to turn on the water heater
the cornstarch I mistake for flour, the disastrous crepes
the cream walls I covered in fabric, in red and green and gold
the center of the iris on the table

dead branches on the beach
dolls in their case for the doll festival, in their silks and reds and golds
the dresses I cannot wear to work
the dreams before the earthquake strikes
the dollar I find in a suitcase

the exhaled breath before a punch in karate class
the friend I have not written to
leftover sushi for breakfast
the monkey that runs across the road, slinging its baby
the narrow alley with its walls
the houses that seem to perch on top
the old man who says 頑張って every morning as I run along the beach
the questions: *How much weight have you lost so far, Sarah-san?*
Why are your eyes green?
rowboat on the beach, Mount Fuji swims in the clouds across the bay
the silences between the words I know and the words I need
typhoon on the roof
the vast crashings of it
young smell of leaves in the rain

the edgy feeling in the eyes when we drive all night
the gash of sun above the islands as we arrive
the hair on the statue, the falling-down
the inscription: Statue of Mother and Child in the Storm
the dome left standing as a memorial, the murdered building
the supports and beams remain, the walls are gone
the thing underneath the blast keeps its structure
like a church if a church had a skeleton

the story in the English textbook at my school
the teacher asks me to read it aloud
One day, a big bomb fell on the city of Hiroshima
the sign above the blackboard says "Move Your Mouth"

I am. I am.

She held him in her arms, just like a little mother

palm trees shift in the sunlight outside the classroom window

Morning came and the sun rose, but the girl never moved again

the children repeat it after me

春 [haru]

Japanese. Spring.

The sun hides under
the days. Lift them away, like wet planks
from a storm-wrecked house.
One removed, two—a breath,
a cry, a light
strikes a smudged, thin face—
and there is the spring, broken, starving,
still alive. Hoist her out.

Princess Moon

In an old, old story, a girl from the moon
appears in a stalk of bamboo,
or in a walnut shell, perhaps in a passion flower.
She dreams of things that spin so slowly
their movement is invisible:
galaxy. Peace. Home.

But her beauty is a torpedo.
Ships and cities and men
explode. She sets them tasks.
Bring me a nail from the Cross.
Bring me a bucket of oil.
Their deaths rest on her skin like pollen.
A suitor stops on a hill
with a cloud.
He builds her body in his mind.
One fingernail escapes. It was there
yesterday. He is terrified.

Midnights, she goes to the mountain.
The moon bangs out its light.
Sometimes she feels a film of sweat
in the palm no one has touched.
The breeze is cold because it leaves so quickly.
The wars are almost over.

Before she vanishes, she writes
the emperor a note. It tells
him how to live forever. He burns it.

The Dark Constellations

The Inca gave the lightless places
names. Fox, toad, serpent. A black
llama with faint eyes.

The space between my hands and the keyboard. I have forgotten how
    the sonata begins.
Photo printed in black and white, so that the wine looks clear.
The mirror in a dark room, waiting for monsters.

In the city sky, the dark animals
have never been; the streetlights erase
what they illuminate.

The pages I ripped from my favorite book when I was two.
The sweatbands on the hats my grandmother gives away
after the funeral, stained with skin and bandannas.
The space between the wedding dress and the small of my back.

We remember the dark animals in dreams;
they are the wind behind us. They are our history.
I don't know where I got this from, we say.

Endurance

The crew learned to sleep
through the grinding: great traffics of ice roaring
through the Antarctic twilight. They learned
to sleep through the whispers of pain, the tiny groans
as the hull pushed back against the ice.
On the night before the water
finally poured like outer space throughout the ship,
a group of penguins mounted an ice floe. They faced
the ship in an arc. And they howled.
All together, their white breasts flung out
toward Shackleton's men, the penguins sang
a long note too thin and steady for grief.
When the ship had gone, the bosun
shot his cat. Shackleton cut three pages
from his Bible and left the rest on the ice.
Black and hunched, the men walked
into the distance. There was no horizon to vanish over.

The Holdout

*Corporal Shoichi Yokoi lived in a cave on the island of Guam
from the end of the Second World War until 1972, when he
was found by a group of hunters.*

He lived in a place of red flowers.
There were birds, and a uniform he made
from hibiscus fibers. His rifle rusted;
his scissors did not. He ate. Breadfruit,
snails, papaya, rat, coconut, eel.
There was a waterfall, and a hill,
and a gap in the stone. Sunlight.
The leaflets fell, then stopped.
Lies. They had not given up.
He swallowed the terrible speech in the brain,
the hibiscus under the fingernails.
He made another shirt.

They greeted him with crowds, with cries in Tokyo.
It is with great embarrassment that I return alive, Yokoi said.

NOTES

All definitions of Japanese words in this text are based on those given in Kim Ahlström, Miwa Ahlström, and Andrew Plummer's *Jisho*, http://jisho.org/.

All definitions of German words in this text are based on those given in *BEOLINGUS—Your Online Dictionary*, TU Chemnitz, http://dict.tu-chemnitz.de/.

The definition for the Greek word ὁδός is based on the one given in Henry George Liddell and Robert Scott, *A Greek-English Lexicon* (Oxford: Clarendon Press, 1940).

Dona nobis pacem translates to "give us peace" and is the text of a traditional canon (song sung in the round).

The line *This is my story . . . This is my song* in the poem "First Week" is quoted from Fanny Crosby and Phoebe Knapp, "Blessed Assurance" (1873).

The line *il pleure dans mon coeur* in the poem "Stimmtausch" is quoted from Paul Verlaine, "Il pleure dans mon coeur," in *Oeuvres complètes de Paul Verlaine*, vol. 1 (Paris: Vanier, 1902).

The poem "Home" quotes from the *Dona nobis pacem* text, the King James translation of the Bible (Luke 15:18, a part of the tale of the Prodigal Son), and an English traditional canon.

The italicized song lyrics in "Inheritance" are quoted from the traditional song "Johnny I Hardly Knew Ye" (Joseph B. Geoghegan, 1867).

Italicized material in the final stanza of the poem "頑張って [ganbatte]" is quoted from *New Horizon English Course 3* (Tokyo: Tokyo Shoseki, 2006).

The penguin episode alluded to in the poem "Endurance" is based in fact; a full account can be found in Caroline Alexander's *The Endurance: Shackleton's Legendary Antarctic Expedition* (New York: Alfred A. Knopf, 2000).

Corporal Shoichi Yokoi's story, and his famous pronouncement upon his return to Japan, are well documented; a full account can be found in Nicholas D. Kristof's "Shoichi Yokoi, 82, Is Dead; Japan Soldier Hid 27 Years," *New York Times*, September 26, 1997.

All errors, of course, are my own.

Wisconsin Poetry Series

Edited by Ronald Wallace and Sean Bishop

How the End First Showed (B) • D. M. Aderibigbe

New Jersey (B) • Betsy Andrews

Salt (B) • Renée Ashley

Horizon Note (B) • Robin Behn

About Crows (FP) • Craig Blais

Mrs. Dumpty (FP) • Chana Bloch

The Declarable Future (4L) • Jennifer Boyden

The Mouths of Grazing Things (B) • Jennifer Boyden

Help Is on the Way (4L) • John Brehm

Sea of Faith (B) • John Brehm

Reunion (FP) • Fleda Brown

Brief Landing on the Earth's Surface (B) • Juanita Brunk

Ejo: Poems, Rwanda, 1991–1994 (FP) • Derick Burleson

Jagged with Love (B) • Susanna Childress

Almost Nothing to Be Scared Of (4L) • David Clewell

The Low End of Higher Things • David Clewell

Now We're Getting Somewhere (FP) • David Clewell

Taken Somehow by Surprise (4L) • David Clewell

Borrowed Dress (FP) • Cathy Colman

Dear Terror, Dear Splendor • Melissa Crowe

Places/Everyone (B) • Jim Daniels

Show and Tell • Jim Daniels

Darkroom (B) • Jazzy Danziger

And Her Soul Out of Nothing (B) • Olena Kalytiak Davis

My Favorite Tyrants (B) • Joanne Diaz

Talking to Strangers (B) • Patricia Dobler

The Golden Coin (4L) • Alan Feldman

(B) = Winner of the Brittingham Prize in Poetry

(FP) = Winner of the Felix Pollak Prize in Poetry

(4L) = Winner of the Four Lakes Prize in Poetry

The Year We Studied Women (FP) • Bruce Snider

Bird Skin Coat (B) • Angela Sorby

The Sleeve Waves (FP) • Angela Sorby

If the House (B) • Molly Spencer

Wait (B) • Alison Stine

Hive (B) • Christina Stoddard

The Red Virgin: A Poem of Simone Weil (B) • Stephanie Strickland

The Room Where I Was Born (B) • Brian Teare

Fragments in Us: Recent and Earlier Poems (FP) • Dennis Trudell

The Apollonia Poems (4L) • Judith Vollmer

Level Green (B) • Judith Vollmer

Reactor • Judith Vollmer

Voodoo Inverso (FP) • Mark Wagenaar

Hot Popsicles • Charles Harper Webb

Liver (FP) • Charles Harper Webb

The Blue Hour (B) • Jennifer Whitaker

Centaur (B) • Greg Wrenn

Pocket Sundial (B) • Lisa Zeidner